What was it like in the past...?

At school

Heinemann
LIBRARY

Sch ... nd Richard Spilsbury

www.heinemann.co.uk/library
Visit our website to find out more information about Heinemann Library books.

To order:

☎ Phone 44 (0) 1865 888066

▤ Send a fax to 44 (0) 1865 314091

▢ Visit the Heinemann Bookshop at www.heinemann.co.uk/library to browse our catalogue and order online.

First published in Great Britain by Heinemann Library, Halley Court, Jordan Hill, Oxford OX2 8EJ, a division of Reed Educational and Professional Publishing Ltd. Heinemann is a registered trademark of Reed Educational & Professional Publishing Ltd.

OXFORD MELBOURNE AUCKLAND JOHANNESBURG BLANTYRE
GABORONE IBADAN PORTSMOUTH (NH) USA CHICAGO

© Reed Educational and Professional Publishing Ltd 2003
The moral right of the proprietor has been asserted.

Designed by Celia Floyd
Originated by Ambassador Litho Ltd
Printed in Hong Kong/China

ISBN 0 431 14828 7   (hardback)   ISBN 0 431 14838 4   (paperback)
07 06 05 04 03   07 06 05 04 03
10 9 8 7 6 5 4 3 2   10 9 8 7 6 5 4 3 2 1

British Library Cataloguing in Publication Data

Spilsbury, Louise
   At school. – (What was it like in the past?)
   1. Schools – History – Juvenile literature
   2. Education – History – Juvenile literature
   I. Title   II. Spilsbury, Richard
   371'.009

Acknowledgements
Quotation on page 19 from 'How we lived then: A history of everyday life during the Second World War' by Norman Longmate, Arrow, 1971.
The Publishers would like to thank the following for permission to reproduce photographs:
Beamish Museum: 8, 9; Camera Press: 27, 29; Corbis: 7, 14, 22; Hulton Archive: 15, 17, 18, 20, 21, 25; Lincoln Local Libraries: 12, 13; Mary Evans: 4, 6, 10; Powerstock Zefa: 5; Topham: 11, 16, 19, 23; Trip: P Wood 24, H Rogers: 26
Cover photograph reproduced with permission of Hulton Archive.

Our thanks to Stuart Copeman for his help in the preparation of this book.
Every effort has been made to contact copyright holders of any material reproduced in this book. Any omissions will be rectified in subsequent printings if notice is given to the Publisher.

Contents

Words printed in **bold letters like these** are explained in the Glossary.

Each **decade** is highlighted on a timeline at the bottom of the page.

Then and now

Is your school building old or new? You may be able to find the date it was built somewhere on the walls, or above the main door.

Look at the photos on these pages. One shows a school built more than 100 years ago. The other school is newer. What differences can you see?

St. Pauls School.   Hammersmith.

This school in Hammersmith, London was built in 1884.

This modern school was built many years after the one in the picture on page 4.

All schools are buildings to teach children in. But there are lots of differences between your school and schools your grandparents or great-grandparents went to.

In this book we look at the ways classrooms, lessons and school life have changed over 100 years.

1900s: Inside schools

In the past many schools had only one or two classrooms. Sometimes children of all ages, from three to thirteen, were taught together in one room. On the walls there would have been just a few pictures, perhaps a map of the world or posters of animals.

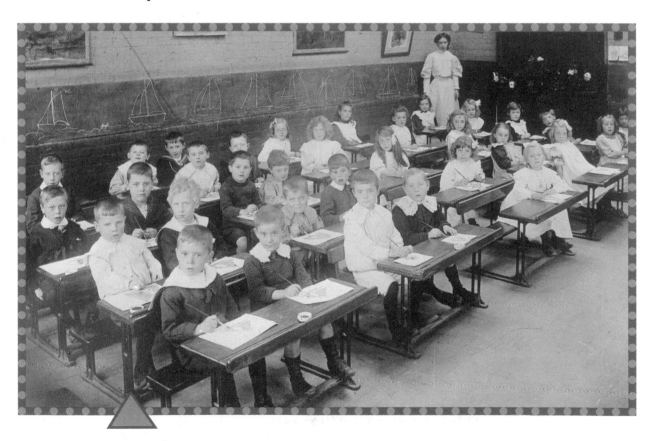

In the 1900s, classrooms had rows of desks for children to sit at.

In the 1900s classrooms could be dark and cold. The **gas lamps** and **oil lanterns** that lit the classrooms were not very bright. In winter, coal fires or **stoves** heated many schools.

Marie Atwill remembers her classroom in 1909: 'It always seemed a cosy room, especially in winter, with a good fire in the grate.'

This shows the inside of a village school in 1902. In the background you can see the stove used to heat the room.

1900s: In the playground

Children had playtimes in the 1900s just as you do today. Some of the games they played then are still played today, like skipping and tag.

Many schools today have special playgrounds and **equipment** to play on. In the 1900s playgrounds were often small, stony yards.

These boys are playing marbles. Have you ever tried this game?

Girls doing 'drill' (PE) in 1905.

When you do PE you probably wear shorts, a t-shirt and trainers. These clothes are easy to stretch and run in. In the 1900s most children wore their ordinary school clothes for PE. These were made of heavy cloth that did not stretch. Girls wore long dresses, pinafores and petticoats.

1910s: Reading and writing

Look around your classroom. How many books can you see? In the 1910s some classes had few books. Children learnt to spell by saying the letters of the words together like this: 'C.A.T. spells CAT. B.A.T. spells BAT.'

Sometimes older children read from a copy of the same book. They took it in turns to stand up and read a page.

The children in this class are lucky because they each have their own book.

In the 1910s most children used slate boards to write on. Slate boards were like small blackboards. You wrote on the board with white chalk. After a teacher checked it, you wiped the slate clean with a damp sponge.

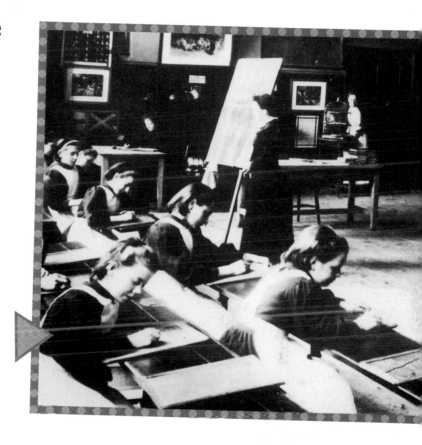

These children are doing their lessons on slate boards.

Some children wrote the letters of the alphabet in sand:
'We spread a thin layer of sand in trays and then formed the letters with our finger. After the teacher inspected them we gave the tray a shake and started all over again.'

1910s: Boys and girls

You probably have a mixture of girls and boys in your class. In the past many schools put older boys and girls in different classes for some lessons.

Boys and girls all learned reading, writing, arithmetic (maths) and **scripture**. Boys also had lessons like **woodwork** and **metalwork**, to help them get a job when they left school.

Only boys had woodwork classes in 1910.

In 1910, some schools taught girls how to iron.

At this time, girls did not have much choice in the jobs they did after school. Some got married and looked after their own house and children. Others went on to be maids. Maids looked after someone else's house and children. Many schools taught girls what they needed to know for these jobs, such as sewing and ironing.

1920s: Getting to school

How do you get to school? In the past, nearly all children walked to school. It did not matter how far away they lived or what the weather was like. There were no school buses and few people had cars. Most children only had one pair of boots. If these were being mended, they could not go to school.

Roads were much quieter in the 1920s, especially country roads like this one.

If they did not have too far to go, children walked home for lunch. If they lived further away, their mums might meet them halfway to give them their food. Most children brought sandwiches to school.

Only a few schools provided dinners in the 1920s.

1930s: School rules

Most classrooms in the 1930s looked the same. Heavy desks with lids were arranged in straight lines. When the teacher talked or wrote on the blackboard, the children had to sit very still and keep very quiet.

If you were naughty or got something wrong, a teacher might smack you on your hand with a wooden ruler.

Children could get into serious trouble if they did not listen to the teacher.

Sir Alec Clegg, a teacher in the 1930s:
'The school day began with prayers followed by **scripture** and **mental arithmetic**... any child getting five out of 20 or less in the daily mental arithmetic test was caned.'

Most children said prayers every morning at school and before meal times.

1940s: City schools

Between 1939 and 1945, Britain was at war with Germany. This was called the Second World War. German planes dropped **bombs** on many towns.

Sometimes school buildings were destroyed. Children had their lessons in other buildings, like churches, hotels or even pubs.

During the Second World War, lessons were often held in buildings like Lacock Abbey, Wiltshire.

The times when bombs were dropped from planes were called **air raids**. To be safe at these times, people went into special **shelters** and teachers often went on giving lessons.

Children squashed inside an air raid shelter. The warden is checking everyone is there.

A girl remembers her school shelter:
'Each child had a tin or box in which we kept two or three comics, a book, some sweets and a favourite toy to keep us occupied during the air raid.'

1940s: Country schools

In the Second World War there were very few **air raids** in the countryside. People sent their children to the country to be safe. This was called evacuation. The children stayed with other families in the country and went to local schools.

Children were often sent away in big groups on trains. How do you think they felt?

Instead of PE, some older children had to help out on local farms.

Lots of country schools became very crowded. Some had 50 or 60 children in a class. Some schools could not fit all the children in at once. Half the pupils came in the morning and the rest came in the afternoon. To save paper they did paintings on old newspapers.

1950s and 1960s: Changes

In the 1950s and 1960s, schools improved. There were usually less than 30 children in a class and they were all the same age.

Schools had electric lights and central heating for the first time. Many had special kitchens, dining halls, gyms and big playing fields.

*Many children wore school **uniforms** in the 1950s.*

1900 1910 1920 1930 1940

This class from 1951 is listening to a radio programme for schoolchildren.

At this time, schoolchildren often listened to radio programmes made for schools. Schools with a television could also watch special TV programmes. These were in black and white, not colour. There were no video recorders, so everyone had to be ready to watch at exactly the right time.

1970s: Creative learning

In the 1900s, children sat quietly in rows of desks facing the teacher. In the 1970s, children sat at low tables in small groups around the classroom. This meant that children could work things out together sometimes. Teachers moved from table to table helping children with their work.

Look at the picture on this page and that on page 7. Now look at your own classroom. What differences can you see?

It was important to learn to read, write and do maths in the 1970s just as it was in the 1900s. But in the 1970s more books were written especially for children. They helped children to learn more easily.

Children also did more painting and model-making. They learnt to play musical instruments and sometimes had dance lessons.

Model-making was a popular (and messy!) activity.

1980s and 1990s: Taking part

Around 100 years ago you learned by repeating things lots of times until you remembered them. Today, you can find things out for yourself.

Teachers take children on trips to zoos, museums or farms. Children sometimes meet and work with theatre and music groups that visit their school.

These children are on a school trip. They are finding out what lives in ponds.

1900 1910 1920 1930 1940

What differences can you see between these uniforms and the ones on page 22?

Today most school **uniforms** are made of stretchy, comfortable material. Some schools let pupils choose whether or not they want to wear uniform. Children also help to make up their class rules. They say how they should behave towards others.

2000s: Schools today

Look at the strange picture on this page. It shows what a French artist in 1900 thought schools would be like in 2000. It shows books being destroyed and machines doing the teaching. Of course, he was wrong in some ways. Schools still use books, but many also have computers in every classroom.

The equipment on the children's heads is a bit like computer headsets of today.

Lots of school children use computers today.

In schools today children use computers to find out lots of things for themselves. They learn from information on the screen which they find on the **Internet**. One day computers may even allow children to feel what it is like to visit planets or to swim with whales in the ocean!

Find out for yourself

There are lots of ways to find out about schools in the past. You could start by asking your parents, grandparents or even your great-grandparents what school was like for them. They may have some old school photographs you can look at.

If your school has a **uniform**, find out when it was designed. Find out what uniforms looked like in the past by looking at old school photographs.

Books

History from Photographs: School, Hodder Wayland, 1999

History Mysteries: At School, A & C Black, 1992

Yesterday and Today: School Days, Franklin Watts, 1998

Glossary

air raids times in war when bombs are dropped on towns and cities

bombs when bombs hit the ground they explode and destroy everything nearby

decade ten years. The decade of the 1910s means the ten years between 1910 and 1920.

equipment playground equipment means things like swings or slides

gas lamps lamps that make light by burning gas to make a flame

Internet ways of finding out lots of information on your computer

mental arithmetic when you do sums in your head

metalwork learning to make things with metal, such as gates

oil lanterns lamps that make light by burning oil to make a flame

scripture lessons about the Bible, the book of Christian people

shelter safe place. Air raid shelters kept people safe from bombs.

stove type of metal firebox in which coal or wood is burned to give off heat

uniform smart clothes that show you belong to a group, such as a particular school

woodwork learning to make things out of wood, such as cupboards

Index